Pedals, Paws, and Papers: Flint Journals Fastest Paperboy!

Marcy Schaaf

Meet Joe, the fastest paperboy in Flint, Michigan! With his trusty bike and a stack of newspapers, Joe's days are filled with exciting deliveries and cheerful waves. But there's one secret to his success: his playful dog, Ogy.

Ogy isn't just any dog–he's a furry bundle of energy with a knack for pulling Joe's bike and making every ride an adventure. Together, they turn a simple paper route into an exhilarating journey full of fun and surprises.

In Pedals, Paws, and Papers: Flint Journal's Fastest Paperboy!, join Joe and Ogy as they zoom through the neighborhood, delivering newspapers and spreading joy. Discover how this dynamic duo shows that with a little creativity and a lot of teamwork, even the most routine tasks can become thrilling adventures. Get ready for a ride that's fast, funny, and full of heart!

Joe loved his bike it was fast and strong.

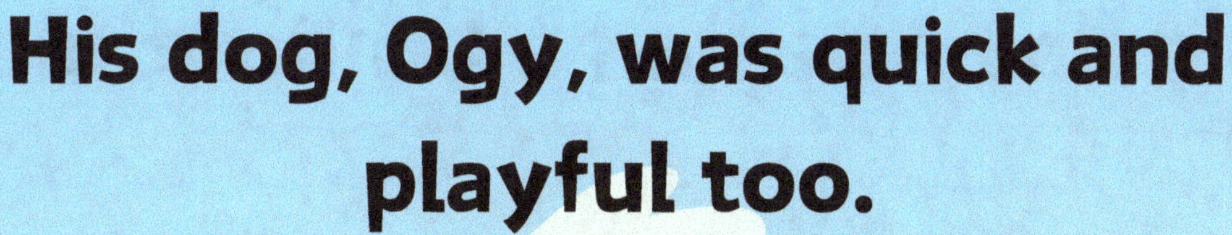

His dog, Ogy, was quick and playful too.

One day, Joe had a brilliant idea.

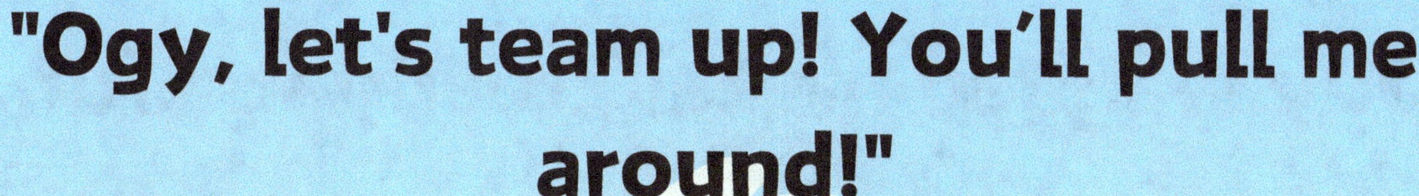
"Ogy, let's team up! You'll pull me around!"

Ogy wagged his tail, ready for fun.

They practiced together in Joe's backyard.

Round and round they went,
faster each time.

Ogy learned to pull Joe without stopping.

"Perfect!" Joe cheered. "Let's visit Franky today!"

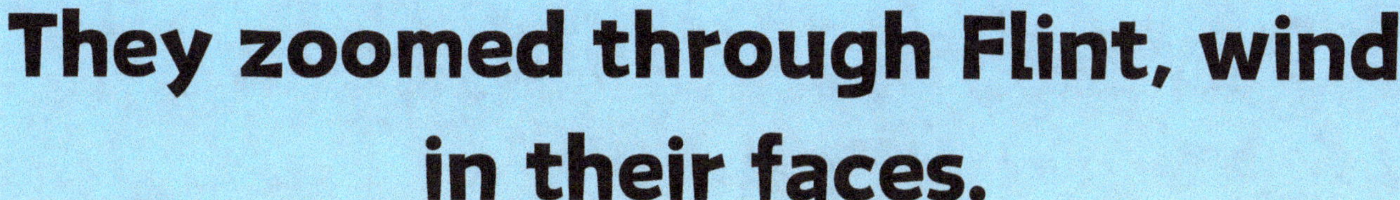

They zoomed through Flint, wind in their faces.

Ogy pulled Joe all the way to Franky's.

Franky laughed, "Cool ride, Joe!
Ogy is awesome!"

Joe grinned, "I trained him myself."

Next, Ogy pulled Joe on his paper route.

Ogy knew every stop, every house by heart.

Papers flew neatly onto porches
as they sped.

Neighbors smiled, impressed by
the team's skills.

Joe knew he could make anything fun.

Even a simple paper route became an adventure.

"Great job, Ogy!" Joe said, handing out papers.

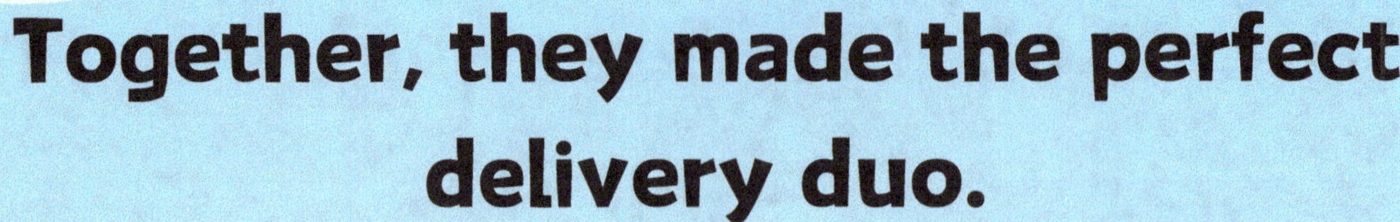

Together, they made the perfect delivery duo.

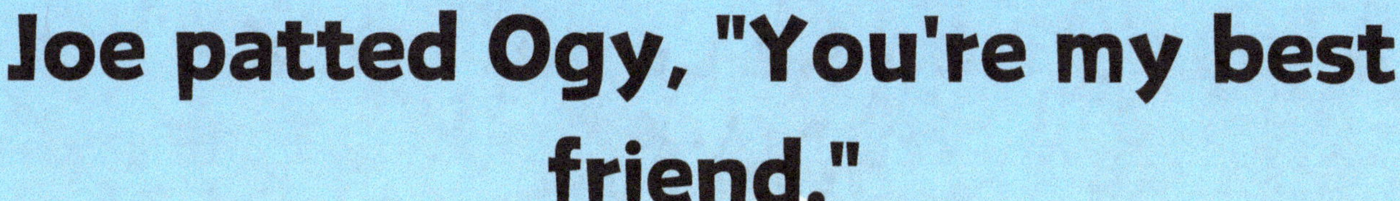

Joe patted Ogy, "You're my best friend."

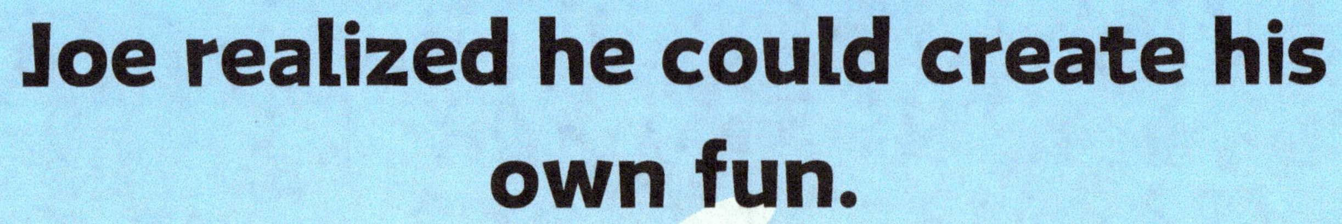
Joe realized he could create his
own fun.

With a bike, a dog, and a plan.

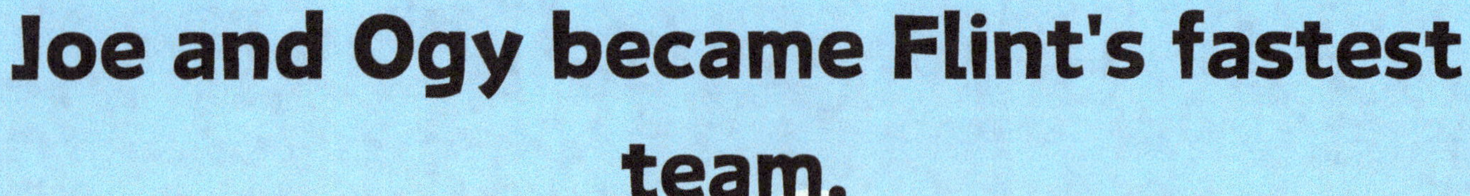

Joe and Ogy became Flint's fastest team.

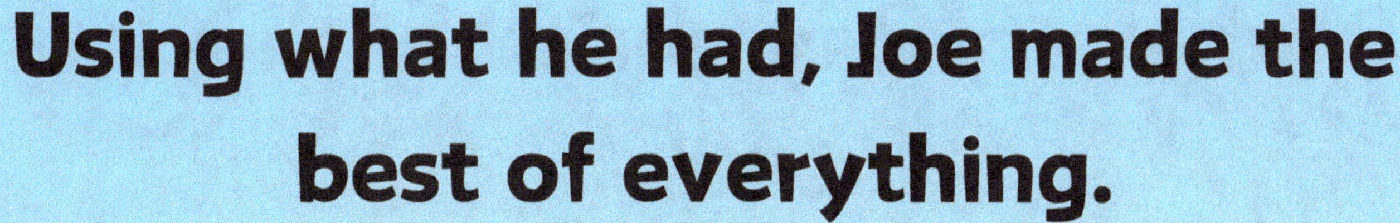

Using what he had, Joe made the best of everything.

And every day ended with a big
smile.

The adventure never stopped for Joe and Ogy.

Books By Schaaf

www.BookBySchaaf.com

Find us at:

Available at
amazon